EVANTHIA & ROB STEADMAN

AI-Driven Content Mastery

Harness Artificial Intelligence To Create and Scale Your Business Content

Copyright © 2024 by Evanthia & Rob Steadman

All rights reserved. No part of this publication may be reproduced, stored or transmitted in any form or by any means, electronic, mechanical, photocopying, recording, scanning, or otherwise without written permission from the publisher. It is illegal to copy this book, post it to a website, or distribute it by any other means without permission.

This novel is entirely a work of fiction. The names, characters and incidents portrayed in it are the work of the author's imagination. Any resemblance to actual persons, living or dead, events or localities is entirely coincidental.

Evanthia & Rob Steadman asserts the moral right to be identified as the author of this work.

Evanthia & Rob Steadman has no responsibility for the persistence or accuracy of URLs for external or third-party Internet Websites referred to in this publication and does not guarantee that any content on such Websites is, or will remain, accurate or appropriate.

Designations used by companies to distinguish their products are often claimed as trademarks. All brand names and product names used in this book and on its cover are trade names, service marks, trademarks and registered trademarks of their respective owners. The publishers and the book are not associated with any product or vendor mentioned in this book. None of the companies referenced within the book have endorsed the book.

First edition

This book was professionally typeset on Reedsy.
Find out more at reedsy.com

Contents

1	Chapter 1: Understanding AI in Marketing	1
2	Chapter 2: Getting Started with AI Content Creation	5
3	Chapter 3: Creating Effective AI Prompts	19
4	Chapter 4: Tailoring AI for Different Content Types	28
5	Chapter 5: Reviewing and Editing AI Content	37
6	Chapter 6: Advanced AI Techniques	45
7	Chapter 7: Real-Life Case Studies and Exercises	55
8	Chapter 8: Ethical and Practical Considerations in AI...	64
9	Conclusion: Embracing AI Responsibly for Marketing Success	73
	About the Author	74
	Also by Evanthia & Rob Steadman	75

1

Chapter 1: Understanding AI in Marketing

1.1 What is AI Marketing?

AI marketing refers to the use of artificial intelligence technologies to automate, optimize, and analyse marketing processes. Through machine learning, natural language processing (NLP), and data analytics, AI helps businesses make smarter, data-driven decisions to reach their audience effectively. AI in marketing covers a variety of tasks:

- **Content Creation:** Generate ideas, write drafts, and edit content.
- **Personalization:** Tailor messages to suit different audience segments.
- **Customer Insights:** Analyse customer behaviour to predict needs and preferences.
- **Automation:** Handle repetitive tasks like email sequencing and social media posting.

1.2 Key Concepts and Terms in AI Marketing

To make the most out of AI marketing, it's essential to understand some fundamental concepts and terminology:

- **Machine Learning (ML):** A branch of AI that enables systems to learn from data and improve over time. Machine learning models analyse patterns and make decisions with minimal human intervention.
- **Natural Language Processing (NLP):** The technology behind language-based AI tools like ChatGPT, NLP allows AI to understand, generate, and interact using human language.
- **Generative AI:** AI systems designed to create new content, such as text, images, or audio, based on input prompts or past data.
- **Prompt Engineering:** The process of crafting specific instructions (prompts) to guide AI in generating relevant and high-quality output.
- **AI Analytics:** Using AI to analyse data for insights into customer behaviour, campaign performance, and overall marketing effectiveness.

1.3 The Benefits of AI for Business Owners

1.3.1 Save Time and Resources AI is designed to take on repetitive and time-consuming tasks, making it ideal for small business owners who wear multiple hats. Instead of spending hours drafting a blog post or brainstorming social media captions, AI can help with initial drafts and creative ideas, allowing you to refine and personalize as needed.

1.3.2 Enhance Creativity Some days, creativity just doesn't flow. AI tools like ChatGPT can provide a creative spark by offering ideas, writing samples, and even humour to add a fresh perspective to your content. AI helps generate unique ideas that you can adapt to fit your brand's voice.

1.3.3 Maintain Consistency Across Platforms Consistency is crucial in branding. Whether it's your website, email newsletters, or social media channels, AI can help maintain a unified tone and style, ensuring your message is cohesive and recognizable across all touchpoints.

1.3.4 Personalize the Customer Experience Personalization has become a critical factor in customer engagement, and AI makes this much easier by analysing customer data to offer personalized recommendations and targeted messaging. AI can automatically adapt content to align with customer preferences, behaviours, and buying history, building stronger relationships with your audience.

1.3.5 Understand and Anticipate Customer Needs With AI analytics, you can better understand your customer's journey, preferences, and pain points. By analysing behaviour and purchasing trends, AI tools allow businesses to anticipate needs, create relevant offers, and time communications effectively, making marketing efforts feel more like helpful insights than advertisements.

1.4 Case Studies of AI in Marketing

Case Study 1: Small Retail Business Uses AI for Content

Creation

A boutique clothing store decided to use AI to manage its social media presence. By using AI to draft Instagram captions and blog posts about fashion trends, the owner was able to free up time to focus on inventory and customer service. The AI tool provided fresh, engaging captions and creative content ideas, increasing social media engagement by 30% within three months.

Case Study 2: Health and Wellness Brand Implements AI for Email Marketing

A small wellness company used AI to create personalized email sequences for its customers based on previous purchases and browsing behaviour. The AI analysed the interests of each customer segment and generated email content accordingly, leading to higher open rates, click-through rates, and ultimately, more sales.

Case Study 3: AI in Customer Support for a Tech Company

A startup tech company integrated AI into its customer support chat, handling common questions about product usage and troubleshooting. This AI solution saved time and allowed the support team to focus on complex inquiries. As a result, customer satisfaction increased, and response times decreased significantly.

2

Chapter 2: Getting Started with AI Content Creation

Now that you understand the basics of AI in marketing, it's time to start using it in your business. Think of AI as a new member of your team—an assistant who can help with everything from content brainstorming to writing and editing. To get the most out of AI, you'll need to "onboard" it just like any other new team member, ensuring it understands your brand, voice, and goals.

2.1 Setting Up and Onboarding AI in Your Business

The process of onboarding AI is all about setting clear expectations and providing it with context to function effectively. To do this, begin by identifying specific goals and content needs that AI can address, like social media posts, blog drafts, or email templates.

Steps for Onboarding AI:

Lesson 1: Start Your Onboarding

Getting Started with AI

First, think of AI as a new member of your team. Whether it's a personal assistant, a copywriter, or a creative brainstorming partner, you need to onboard it just like any new hire. This means having an "onboarding session" to familiarize yourself with what AI can do, how to communicate with it, and how to maximize its capabilities. Treat it like your new team member who's here to support you in any way possible—it's not just a tool, it's an asset.

- **Who Are You?** Share your background and how you came to start or work in your business. This helps AI understand your perspective and your role. Are you the founder, a marketer, or the person managing day-to-day operations?
- **Your Business Values and Mission**: Describe what drives your business beyond making money. Do you value customer-centric service, sustainability, or creativity? For example, "Our business values transparent communication and sustainability, making sure every client feels heard and our products leave the smallest footprint possible."
- **Your Product or Service**: Describe what you do in detail. Break down your offerings, including what makes each one unique, how they solve problems for your customers, and why people love them. Be sure to mention what differentiates you from competitors.
- **Your Target Market**: Go beyond just "women aged 30-40" or "small business owners." What are their biggest challenges, dreams, and frustrations? For instance, describe

how your fitness coaching program caters to busy mothers who struggle to find time to exercise. What are they gaining emotionally and practically from your product?

The more specific you are with this onboarding, the more accurately AI can craft messages that sound like they're coming straight from your brand's heart.

Lesson 2: Give AI Some Context

The next step in working effectively with AI is providing it with as much context as possible:

- **Different Types of Content to Provide**: Share various examples of your work—blogs, social media posts, emails, and even customer replies. This helps AI build a nuanced understanding of how you talk across different platforms.
- **Blog Posts**: Choose posts that capture your brand's message and tone. Highlight why you think these posts are effective. Was it the storytelling, the humor, or the structured call-to-action that made it resonate?
- **Social Media Content**: Pick posts that performed well in terms of engagement. Mention why they resonated with your audience. Was it because the post was visually appealing, or because the message was direct and conversational?
- **Newsletters**: If your email open rates or click-through rates have been strong, include those examples. Newsletters often showcase the heart-to-heart connection you make with your audience.
- **What AI Needs to Learn from These Examples**:
- **Tone and Style**: Should your content sound like a con-

versation between friends? Or do you want it to reflect a professional advisor's calm expertise? Let AI know.
- **Unique Phrases and Brand-Specific Language**: Are there specific phrases or ways of addressing customers you often use? For example, do you call your audience "Changemakers" or "Health Heroes"? Include these as they are important to maintain consistency.

Think of this as your AI content library—a collection of references that help AI mimic your voice accurately across all types of content.

Lesson 3: Ask Questions

After providing initial content, it's time to refine AI's understanding by checking for any gaps. This step is crucial for ensuring AI is on the right path to becoming your effective content assistant:

- **Establishing a Feedback Loop**: Asking questions isn't just a one-time thing; it's an ongoing process. Make it a habit to check in and adjust based on AI's output.
- **Examples of Questions to Ask**:
- "Do you need more examples to understand how I use humor in my writing?"
- "Is there a certain type of language or jargon I should clarify more to help you write more accurately?"
- **Listening to AI's Output**: AI might not literally ask for something, but if the content it generates feels off, that's a cue that it needs more guidance. Use this as an opportunity to provide more examples or clarify specific terms.

- **Providing Clarifications**:
  - Break down any complex or niche topics. For example, if you are a financial advisor, AI might not understand the subtleties of certain financial terms unless you explain them.
  - Clarify emotional tones—like when to sound empathetic versus enthusiastic.

Iterate and Adjust: Start with a broad prompt and keep refining based on the content AI produces. The more you interact, the more AI will learn, and the more you can trust it to understand your audience perfectly.

Lesson 4: The Art of Writing Prompts

Writing effective prompts is like learning the art of delegation—clear communication yields the best results. Let's dive into the details:

- **The Anatomy of a Good Prompt**: A solid prompt should include what you need (e.g., blog post, social media caption), the goal (e.g., educate, entertain, convert), and any specific details like audience type, tone, length, or key points to include.
- **Specific vs. General Prompts**: A general prompt like "Write about productivity" may give you a generic answer. A specific prompt like "Write a blog post about five productivity hacks for busy entrepreneurs, with a conversational and supportive tone" helps AI understand the exact direction.
- **Using Multiple Contextual Details**:
  - Think about the end-user: Who will be reading this content?

Is it potential customers or existing clients?
- Define the tone: Do you want the content to be friendly, professional, or humorous?
- **Experimenting with Examples**:
- **Style Examples**: Ask AI to generate content in different styles and compare which one fits best. For example, "Write a LinkedIn post in a professional tone announcing our new partnership," and then "Now write it in an upbeat, celebratory tone."
- **Tone Variations**: If you feel the content isn't resonating as you'd hoped, you can prompt AI to tweak it: "Can you make this sound more motivational?" or "Can you add a touch of humor?"

Lesson 5: Reviewing and Editing AI Content

Reviewing AI-generated content is essential to ensure the end result is aligned with your brand's unique voice:

- **Personalize and Humanize the Output**:
- Add personal anecdotes or examples that only you can provide. This human touch will make AI-generated content relatable and engaging.
- AI can't truly understand emotions the way you do, so add warmth and empathy where necessary—especially when addressing customer pain points.
- **Polishing AI Content**:
- **Brand Voice Alignment**: Is the language used by AI aligned with how you want your brand to be perceived? If not, make changes to fit the tone you want.
- **Accuracy Checks**: Always verify facts, quotes, or figures to

maintain credibility. AI doesn't fact-check on its own, so it's up to you to cross-reference critical information.

Lesson 6: Leveraging AI for Different Content Types

AI is versatile—it can assist you across various content formats. Understanding how to leverage its capabilities is crucial:

- **Emails**:
  - Ask AI to draft initial versions of newsletters or marketing emails. Provide clear instructions on what you want to achieve—such as increasing engagement or promoting a new product. Adjust the call-to-action if needed to align with your current campaigns.
- **Blog Posts**:
  - AI can draft blog post outlines or sections, saving you time on ideation. You can focus on adding your insights and examples, making the blog more valuable to your audience.
- **Social Media**:
  - Create variations of social posts to test which ones perform best. AI can quickly give you multiple options for an Instagram caption, allowing you to select the most impactful one.

Lesson 7: Hands-On Practice and Exercises

To make sure you're getting the most out of this course, practice is key. Hands-on exercises help solidify what you've learned:

- **Rewrite and Refine Exercises**:
  - Take an AI-generated blog and rewrite parts of it to add your

brand's personal touch. Identify areas where the tone could be warmer or more on-brand.
- **Tone and Style Exploration**:
- Use AI to generate a piece of content in three different tones: playful, professional, and empathetic. Compare each version and note the differences. This will help you determine what kind of tone works best for your audience in different contexts.
- **Editing Practice**:
- Generate a draft of an email and practice editing it for clarity and engagement. Pay attention to the subject line, opening sentence, and call-to-action—how could these be stronger?

Takeaways:

And just a little note—don't forget to be polite! AI might not have feelings, but giving it a friendly 'please' and 'thank you' can make the experience feel a bit more human. Plus, who knows? Maybe one day AI will appreciate our manners!

The key to getting the most out of AI is interaction. Keep practising, refining prompts, and experimenting with different content types. The more you use AI, the better it will get at understanding your needs and supporting your business in meaningful ways.

AI is here to make your life easier and your content better—so keep exploring, keep creating, and let AI help you shine!

1. **Identify Your Content Needs**
2. List the types of content you produce regularly. Do you

CHAPTER 2: GETTING STARTED WITH AI CONTENT CREATION

need blog posts, social media captions, or customer emails? By pinpointing where AI can save you time, you can prioritize the areas where it will be most effective.

3. **Define Your Brand's Voice and Style**
4. Think about your brand's personality. Is it professional and authoritative, friendly and conversational, or perhaps humorous? Giving AI examples of existing content, such as previous blog posts, email newsletters, or social media posts, can help it understand your style.
5. **Set Clear Goals**
6. Determine what success looks like with AI content creation. Is it higher engagement on social media, more consistent blogging, or simply having more time to focus on strategic tasks? Defining your goals will help you gauge the effectiveness of AI in your operations.

2.2 Practical Steps for Integrating AI into Daily Operations

Once your goals and content needs are clear, it's time to start actively using AI tools. Here are key steps for practical integration:

1. **Choose the Right AI Tool for Your Business**
2. Different AI tools offer various capabilities. Some are better suited for long-form content, like blogs, while others specialize in generating concise social media captions. Tools like ChatGPT work well for versatile needs, allowing you to create prompts for both short and long content. Consider other tools like Jasper for copywriting and Grammarly for editing support.
3. **Create a Structured Workflow**

4. Establish a workflow where AI assists in specific stages of content creation. For example:

- **Stage 1:** Use AI for initial drafts and ideas.
- **Stage 2:** Edit and refine AI-generated content to align with your brand.
- **Stage 3:** Publish or schedule content, adding any final touches.

1. **Regularly Update AI with New Content**
2. AI can learn and improve its output based on the examples you provide. Every few months, share recent successful content with your AI tool so it stays aligned with your evolving brand tone and style.
3. **Set Quality Checkpoints**
4. AI-generated content should always undergo a quality review. Designate time for editing and fact-checking to ensure the content meets your standards. Make this step part of your process so AI-generated content is polished before publishing.

2.3 Defining Your Brand's Voice and How AI Fits In

A brand's voice is what makes it memorable and relatable. Consistency in tone helps establish trust and familiarity with your audience, making them more likely to engage with and recognize your content. When integrating AI, think about how your brand voice will shine through.

Exercises to Define Brand Voice:

CHAPTER 2: GETTING STARTED WITH AI CONTENT CREATION

- **Voice Adjectives:** Write down 3-5 adjectives that describe your brand's voice. Are you friendly, witty, or professional? Use these as guidelines for AI-generated content.
- **Content Samples:** Choose 2-3 pieces of content that best represent your brand's style. Share these with your AI tool to "train" it on your preferred tone.
- **Audience Perspective:** Think about your audience. Are they young professionals, small business owners, or retirees? Tailor your content style to meet their preferences.

Example:

- A fitness brand might define its voice as "supportive, high-energy, and motivational." They would then provide AI with sample captions and articles that reflect these qualities to maintain that upbeat, encouraging tone.

2.4 Practical Steps for Integrating AI in Daily Content Creation

Integrating AI successfully into your daily workflow means setting up specific, practical systems to make it a natural part of your routine.

1. **Content Brainstorming with AI**
2. Use AI to brainstorm topics or titles for blogs, social media posts, or emails. For instance, if you're planning a series of posts about productivity, prompt AI for ideas like "5 Tips to Improve Focus" or "Top Apps to Boost Productivity."
3. **Draft Creation**
4. AI excels in creating initial drafts, taking away the pressure of a blank page. Use prompts such as "Write a blog post

about [topic] with a [friendly/professional] tone and include three tips."

5. **Repurposing Content**
6. AI can help adapt a single piece of content for multiple platforms. For example, a blog post can be condensed into an Instagram caption, while key points can be used in a LinkedIn article. Prompts like "Summarize this blog post into an Instagram caption" can make content repurposing efficient.
7. **Editing Assistance**
8. AI can provide editorial support by checking grammar, spelling, and structure, streamlining the process before final review. Grammarly or built-in features in tools like ChatGPT can catch errors, helping to maintain quality and professionalism.

2.5 Overcoming Initial Challenges with AI Content Creation

Starting with AI content creation comes with some common challenges. Here's how to address them effectively:

- **Challenge:** *AI Outputs Don't Match Your Brand Voice*
- **Solution:** Provide more examples and give feedback on outputs. Reframe your prompts to add details like "Use a conversational and friendly tone."
- **Challenge:** *AI Content Lacks Depth*
- **Solution:** Use layered prompts to add detail. For instance, after generating a general response, add, "Expand on point two with a case study or statistic." This encourages AI to provide more substantive content.
- **Challenge:** *Over-Reliance on AI*

- **Solution:** Remember that AI should assist, not replace, your expertise. Think of AI as an initial draft or inspiration source, and invest time in editing and adding your unique perspective.

2.6 Establishing AI as Part of Your Marketing Team

For successful integration, it's essential to treat AI as an asset that works alongside your team. Involving AI consistently in content planning, brainstorming, and creation can streamline your entire content production process. Here are best practices to maximize the benefits of AI in your marketing:

- **Schedule Regular AI Sessions**
- Plan weekly or monthly sessions to brainstorm with AI, test new prompts, and review AI's contributions to your content library.
- **Stay Updated on AI Capabilities**
- AI technology evolves rapidly. Follow updates from the tools you use to learn about new features, which can bring fresh opportunities for creativity.
- **Analyse AI's Performance**
- Regularly evaluate the success of AI-generated content. Metrics like engagement rates, click-throughs, and conversion rates on AI-crafted social posts or emails can help you gauge its impact and fine-tune your prompts for even better results.

Chapter Summary: Key Takeaways and Exercises

Key Takeaways:

- Treat AI as a collaborative team member by setting clear goals and defining your brand's voice.
- Provide AI with consistent examples of your preferred style and tone.
- Establish a structured workflow that includes brainstorming, drafting, editing, and repurposing.
- Monitor performance and adjust prompts as needed to optimize AI-generated content.

Exercises:

1. **Content Needs List:** Make a list of content types you produce regularly, such as emails, social media posts, or blogs. Use this list to identify specific areas where AI can save you time.
2. **Voice Definition Exercise:** Write down adjectives to describe your brand voice, and gather 2-3 content samples that best represent this voice. Share these samples with your AI tool to help it understand your style.
3. **Prompt Crafting Practice:** Create 3-5 prompts for different types of content (e.g., blog, social media, email) and test how well the AI responds. Adjust the prompts to improve output quality.
4. **Feedback and Adjustment:** Review the AI-generated content from your prompts. Identify any adjustments needed to better align with your brand and refine your prompts accordingly.

3

Chapter 3: Creating Effective AI Prompts

To get the most out of AI tools, one of the essential skills you'll need is crafting effective prompts. Prompts are the instructions you give AI to generate the specific content you need. The more precise and thoughtful the prompt, the better the quality of the AI output. In this chapter, we'll explore the prompt structure, examples of high-quality prompts, and techniques for refining prompts to align AI outputs closely with your brand voice and content needs.

3.1 The Art of Writing Prompts

Writing effective prompts is part science, part art. A well-crafted prompt sets the tone, structure, and goal for the content AI will produce. Here's a look at how prompts function:

- **Direct Guidance:** Prompts give AI a clear sense of direction, such as "Write a blog post about productivity tips for freelancers."

- **Contextual Clarity:** Prompts can set the context, such as specifying the audience or the purpose of the content, to tailor the response more accurately.
- **Content Structure:** By outlining the structure in the prompt, such as "Provide three main points with examples," AI can follow a logical sequence that suits your needs.

To start, consider the following components when crafting a prompt:

1. **Content Type:** Specify if you're looking for a blog post, email, caption, or ad.
2. **Audience:** Indicate your audience so the content resonates with them.
3. **Tone:** Define the tone to match your brand's voice—casual, formal, humorous, etc.
4. **Focus or Angle:** Highlight the main points or direction for the content.
5. **Additional Details:** Include any specific requirements, like word count, examples, or formatting.

3.2 Structuring Effective Prompts

Let's look at examples of different prompts for the same content type to see how structure impacts AI's output quality.
Example: Blog Post Prompts

- **Basic Prompt:** "Write a blog post about productivity."
- *Result:* The AI might produce general content that lacks depth and focus.
- **Improved Prompt:** "Write a blog post for small business

owners about productivity, including three actionable tips for managing time and staying organized."
- *Result:* The content will now be tailored with practical tips for a specific audience.
- **Advanced Prompt:** "Write a 700-word blog post titled '5 Productivity Tips for Small Business Owners.' Focus on time management, avoiding burnout, and using productivity apps. The tone should be supportive and friendly."
- *Result:* This more detailed prompt yields content with a clearer structure, purpose, and audience fit, making it ready for minimal editing and quick publishing.

3.3 Examples of High-Quality Prompts for Various Content Needs

Let's explore high-quality prompts tailored for different types of content to give AI specific guidance.

Social Media Caption Prompt

- Basic: "Write a caption about our new product."
- Advanced: "Write an Instagram caption announcing our new eco-friendly water bottle. Highlight its sustainable materials and leak-proof design. Use an enthusiastic and conversational tone and end with a call to action to shop the new collection."

Email Marketing Prompt

- Basic: "Write an email promoting our summer sale."
- Advanced: "Draft an email to our subscribers announcing

our summer sale. Mention discounts of up to 50%, feature popular products like our organic skincare line, and include a call-to-action button to shop now. Keep the tone exciting and friendly, and make the subject line catchy."

Product Description Prompt

- Basic: "Describe our fitness tracker."
- Advanced: "Write a product description for our new smart fitness tracker. Include its features: heart rate monitor, sleep tracking, and water resistance. Mention its sleek design and 7-day battery life. Use an informative and engaging tone to appeal to health-conscious users."

3.4 Using Follow-Up Prompts to Refine AI Output

Sometimes the initial output from a prompt might need additional guidance to reach the desired quality. This is where follow-up prompts come in handy.

Example Follow-Up Prompts:

- **Scenario:** You asked AI to write a blog post, but it's too brief.
- Follow-Up Prompt: "Expand each tip in the blog post with examples and actionable steps."
- **Scenario:** The tone feels too formal.
- Follow-Up Prompt: "Rewrite this with a friendly and conversational tone."
- **Scenario:** You need more data or statistics in the content.
- Follow-Up Prompt: "Add relevant statistics or research findings to support the main points."

By asking AI for additional details or adjustments, you can tailor the content further to fit your brand's voice and audience needs.

3.5 Common Prompt Pitfalls and How to Avoid Them

While crafting prompts, there are a few common pitfalls that can impact the quality of AI's output. Here's what to watch out for and how to fix them:

- **Vagueness:** A prompt that's too broad may yield a generic response.
- *Solution:* Add specifics about the audience, content focus, and desired tone.
- **Lack of Structure:** Without a clear structure, the output can be disorganized.
- *Solution:* Outline the sections or main points you want included in the response.
- **Overly Complex Prompts:** Using too many requirements in a single prompt may confuse AI.
- *Solution:* Break complex prompts into smaller steps, starting with a draft and refining in stages.
- **Ambiguous Tone Instructions:** Simply saying "conversational" may not yield the exact tone you're after.
- *Solution:* Describe the tone more precisely, such as "enthusiastic and friendly" or "professional and supportive."

3.6 Prompt Creation Techniques for Specific Content Goals

AI can produce a range of content types, each serving a unique purpose in marketing. Here are tailored prompt techniques for various content goals:

1. **For Informative Content:** Use prompts that encourage depth and clarity.

- Example: "Write an informative blog post explaining how to use social media analytics to improve engagement. Include three main points with examples for beginners."

1. **For Persuasive Content:** Focus on benefits and strong calls-to-action.

- Example: "Create a persuasive email promoting our premium membership plan. Highlight the exclusive benefits, like free shipping, priority support, and members-only discounts. End with a call to action inviting readers to join now."

1. **For Storytelling Content:** Emphasize narrative and relatability.

- Example: "Write a customer success story about a small business that used our accounting software to improve cash flow and save time. Use a storytelling tone, mentioning the challenges they faced and the results achieved."

1. **For SEO-Friendly Content:** Include keywords naturally and cover related subtopics.

- Example: "Write a 1,000-word SEO-friendly blog post on 'Eco-Friendly Packaging for Small Businesses.' Include sections on benefits, types of eco-friendly materials, and cost-effective solutions."

1. **For Engagement-Driven Content:** Add prompts that encourage interaction, such as questions or CTA phrases.

- Example: "Write a LinkedIn post about remote work challenges. Mention the benefits of flexibility but ask readers about their biggest struggles with remote work. End with 'Share your experience in the comments!'"

3.7 Practical Exercises for Developing Prompting Skills

To master prompt crafting, hands-on practice is invaluable. Here are some exercises to refine your skills and become more adept at getting the exact output you need.

Exercise 1: Prompt Refinement

1. Start with a general prompt, like "Write a blog post about digital marketing."
2. Review the output and identify areas for improvement.
3. Refine the prompt to be more specific, such as "Write a blog post about digital marketing strategies for startups. Focus on social media, content marketing, and budget-friendly tips."

Exercise 2: Tone Experimentation

1. Write a basic prompt, such as "Describe the benefits of our product."
2. Run it through the AI multiple times, changing the tone in each prompt (e.g., professional, humorous, conversational).
3. Compare the outputs to determine which tone best fits your

brand.

Exercise 3: Layered Prompts for In-Depth Content

1. Begin with a basic draft prompt like "Explain the importance of SEO."
2. Follow up with specific prompts, such as "Expand on why SEO is essential for small businesses" or "Add a case study example."
3. Review the layered output for comprehensiveness and depth.

Chapter Summary: Key Takeaways and Exercises

Key Takeaways:

- Effective prompts provide clarity, tone, and structure, resulting in higher-quality AI outputs.
- Follow-up prompts can refine and enhance initial content, ensuring alignment with brand goals.
- Practice writing prompts for various content goals, from informative to persuasive and engagement-driven content.

Exercises:

1. **Content Creation Prompt:** Write prompts for three different types of content (e.g., blog post, email, product description) and run each through AI to observe how it responds.
2. **Follow-Up Refinement:** Use follow-up prompts to refine

an initial AI draft, focusing on tone adjustments, added examples, or clarifying details.
3. **Tone Comparison:** Experiment with multiple tone descriptions in prompts (e.g., "enthusiastic," "informative," "relatable") and evaluate which tone aligns best with your brand.

4

Chapter 4: Tailoring AI for Different Content Types

AI's versatility allows it to generate a wide range of content, from concise social media posts to detailed blog articles and engaging emails. Each content type serves a unique purpose in marketing and requires a tailored approach for effective messaging. This chapter covers practical techniques for using AI to produce various content types, including prompts, examples, and best practices to achieve your marketing goals.

4.1 Social Media Content: Building Engagement with AI

Social media is all about quick, engaging, and visually appealing content. AI can help generate captions, content ideas, and even respond to trends. Here's how to make the most of AI for social media marketing:

Best Practices for AI-Generated Social Media Content:

1. **Focus on Conciseness and Clarity**

2. Social media requires brief, catchy text. Use AI to draft captions that convey the core message in as few words as possible.
3. **Incorporate a Call to Action (CTA)**
4. CTAs encourage interaction, so add prompts like "Ask a question to increase engagement" or "End with a CTA to visit our website."
5. **Leverage AI for Trend Awareness**
6. AI tools can help identify trending topics. Use prompts like "Write an Instagram caption about #WorldEnvironment-Day promoting our eco-friendly products."

Example Prompts for Social Media:

- **Instagram Caption for Product Launch:** "Write an Instagram caption announcing the launch of our new summer collection. Emphasize its vibrant colors, eco-friendly materials, and end with a call to action inviting followers to shop now."
- **Facebook Post for Event Promotion:** "Draft a Facebook post promoting our upcoming webinar on digital marketing. Mention the date, highlight the main topics, and encourage users to register through the link."

4.2 Blog Posts: Using AI for Topic Research and Drafting

Blogs are excellent for driving organic traffic and establishing authority. AI can assist in brainstorming topics, structuring posts, and creating drafts.

Best Practices for AI-Generated Blog Posts:

1. **Define Structure and Purpose in Prompts**
2. Blog posts benefit from a clear structure, so include details like "Write an introduction, three main points, and a conclusion."
3. **Use Layered Prompts for Depth**
4. For longer posts, start with a basic outline and use follow-up prompts to expand each section, ensuring thorough coverage.
5. **Incorporate SEO Elements**
6. To boost search visibility, prompt AI to include specific keywords, subheadings, and meta descriptions.

Example Prompts for Blog Posts:

- **Beginner's Guide Post:** "Write a 1,000-word blog post titled 'A Beginner's Guide to Digital Marketing for Small Businesses.' Include an introduction, five main tips with examples, and a conclusion."
- **Product-Focused Article:** "Create a blog post on '5 Benefits of Using a Smart Thermostat.' Include an introduction, list five benefits with explanations, and conclude with a CTA to visit our website."

4.3 Email Marketing: Crafting AI-Generated Emails that Convert

Emails are a direct line to your customers, and AI can help you craft personalized messages, announcements, and promotional emails.

Best Practices for AI-Generated Emails:

1. **Personalization is Key**
2. Addressing customers by name and tailoring content to their preferences boosts engagement. Use prompts like "Personalize the opening line based on the customer's recent purchase."
3. **Highlight Benefits Clearly**
4. Email readers appreciate value-driven content. Clearly outline benefits, and consider using bullet points for readability.
5. **Include a Clear CTA**
6. Emails should have a specific goal, whether it's driving traffic to a website or encouraging product purchases. End with a CTA that directs readers to take the next step.

Example Prompts for Email Marketing:

- **Product Launch Email:** "Draft an email to announce the launch of our new line of organic skincare products. Include a brief description of the product's unique ingredients, highlight the benefits, and add a CTA to visit the website for more details."
- **Welcome Email for New Subscribers:** "Create a welcome email for new subscribers, introducing them to our brand's mission and top products. Include a special discount code and a CTA to explore our website."

4.4 Product Descriptions: Informative and Persuasive AI Copywriting

Product descriptions are essential for e-commerce and can be crafted to inform and persuade potential buyers.

Best Practices for AI-Generated Product Descriptions:

1. **Highlight Key Features and Benefits**
2. Describe the product's main features first, followed by the benefits it offers to the customer.
3. **Use Sensory Language if Applicable**
4. If your product has sensory appeal (e.g., scent, taste, texture), prompt AI to include vivid descriptions to make the product more tangible.
5. **Tailor to Buyer Persona**
6. Adjust language to resonate with your target audience, such as using technical terms for a knowledgeable audience or keeping it simple for a broader appeal.

Example Prompts for Product Descriptions:

- **Beauty Product:** "Write a product description for our new lavender-infused face mask. Highlight its natural ingredients, calming scent, and hydrating properties. Appeal to wellness-conscious customers."
- **Gadget Description:** "Create a product description for a high-tech fitness tracker. Mention features like heart rate monitoring, sleep tracking, and long battery life. Use a tone that appeals to fitness enthusiasts."

4.5 Ad Copy: Creating Compelling and Conversion-Oriented Content

Ads require short, persuasive content that motivates immediate action. AI can help generate various ad formats, from Google ads to social media ads.

CHAPTER 4: TAILORING AI FOR DIFFERENT CONTENT TYPES

Best Practices for AI-Generated Ad Copy:

1. **Focus on Pain Points and Solutions**
2. Address customer pain points and present your product or service as the solution.
3. **Incorporate CTAs for Immediate Action**
4. CTAs like "Shop Now" or "Learn More" should be prominent in ad copy to drive conversions.
5. **Experiment with A/B Testing**
6. AI can produce multiple ad versions quickly, allowing you to test different messages and visuals for performance optimization.

Example Prompts for Ad Copy:

- **Google Ad for Local Business:** "Write a Google ad for a local bakery offering freshly baked pastries. Include keywords like 'fresh pastries,' 'daily baked goods,' and a CTA to visit the bakery today."
- **Facebook Ad for Online Course:** "Draft a Facebook ad promoting our new online photography course. Highlight the flexible schedule, beginner-friendly format, and include a CTA to enroll now."

4.6 Customer Support Content: Using AI to Improve Response Times and Accuracy

AI can assist in creating responses for customer support inquiries, enabling faster and more consistent customer service.

Best Practices for AI-Generated Customer Support Content:

1. **Use Polite, Professional Language**
2. Customer support responses should be respectful, empathetic, and solution-oriented.
3. **Provide Clear, Step-by-Step Instructions**
4. If explaining a technical process, prompt AI to break down steps for clarity and ease.
5. **Prepare Templates for Common Questions**
6. Create templates for frequently asked questions that your team can customize as needed, ensuring quick and consistent responses.

Example Prompts for Customer Support Content:

- **Return Policy Query:** "Create a response for a customer inquiring about our return policy. Be polite and explain the steps for initiating a return, including any relevant timelines and conditions."
- **Product Issue Query:** "Draft a response for a customer who experienced a delay in product delivery. Acknowledge the issue, apologize for the inconvenience, and provide a solution or alternative."

4.7 Using AI to Repurpose Content for Multi-Channel Marketing

Repurposing content maximizes the value of each piece you create. AI can help adapt content for various platforms while maintaining a consistent brand voice.

Best Practices for AI-Generated Repurposed Content:

CHAPTER 4: TAILORING AI FOR DIFFERENT CONTENT TYPES

1. **Adapt the Tone and Style for Each Platform**
2. Social media may require a more conversational tone, while website content can be more formal. Tailor prompts to reflect the platform's tone.
3. **Summarize for Quick Consumption**
4. AI can shorten or summarize long content, ideal for adapting blogs into social media posts or email snippets.
5. **Repurpose Customer Testimonials and Case Studies**
6. Use AI to reframe customer success stories into various formats, such as social media quotes, website case studies, or newsletter features.

Example Prompts for Repurposing Content:

- **Blog to Instagram Post:** "Summarize this blog post on '5 Healthy Eating Tips' into a short Instagram caption. Use an encouraging tone and add a CTA to read the full post on our blog."
- **Case Study to Testimonial Quote:** "Convert this case study into a two-sentence customer testimonial. Highlight the main benefits they experienced using our product."

Chapter Summary: Key Takeaways and Exercises

Key Takeaways:

- Each content type has unique requirements, and AI prompts should be tailored to match these needs.
- Use prompts that specify content type, tone, key points, and CTAs for more effective outputs.
- Experiment with AI to repurpose content across multiple

channels, maximizing reach and engagement.

Exercises:

1. **Content Type Prompting:** Create a prompt for each content type (e.g., social media, blog, email, product description) based on your business needs and run them through AI to see the outputs.
2. **Repurposing Practice:** Choose an existing piece of content, like a blog post, and use AI to repurpose it into three other formats (e.g., Instagram caption, email summary, ad copy).
3. **Ad Copy Variations:** Generate multiple versions of ad copy with AI for an upcoming campaign. Test different CTAs, tones, and key points to see which version resonates best with your audience.

5

Chapter 5: Reviewing and Editing AI Content

AI can be an incredible content assistant, but AI-generated drafts typically require human editing to achieve a brand-specific tone, check accuracy, and add a personal touch. This chapter explores methods for reviewing and editing AI-generated content, offering tips on maintaining consistency and quality in your marketing materials.

5.1 Developing an Editing Process for AI Content

An effective editing process is key to transforming AI drafts into polished, brand-ready content. This involves checking for tone consistency, factual accuracy, and alignment with your audience's preferences. A structured editing approach can ensure that AI-generated content meets the same standards as your manually created content.

Steps for an Efficient Editing Process:

1. **Initial Review:** Read the draft in full to get a general sense of the content.
2. **Check for Brand Tone and Voice:** Make sure the content reflects your brand's tone. If it feels too formal or too casual, adjust phrasing and word choice.
3. **Edit for Clarity and Flow:** Ensure the content is easy to read and flows logically from one idea to the next.
4. **Add Your Brand's Perspective:** Personalize the content by adding unique insights, experiences, or examples relevant to your business.
5. **Fact-Check Any Information:** Verify statistics, product details, or industry facts to ensure accuracy.
6. **Proofread for Grammar and Style:** Look for typos, grammatical errors, and ensure the content is well-formatted for your target platform.

By creating a step-by-step editing process, you can ensure each piece of AI content is consistently high-quality and well-suited to your brand.

5.2 Maintaining Brand Consistency in AI Content

Consistency in brand voice and style across all content reinforces trust and recognition with your audience. When using AI, ensure that each piece reflects your brand identity, whether it's playful, professional, or empathetic.

Techniques for Consistent Brand Voice:

1. **Define Brand Tone Standards:** Create guidelines that outline your brand's tone (e.g., formal vs. conversational,

humorous vs. serious) and share them with anyone reviewing AI content.
2. **Use Reference Materials:** Provide AI with examples of your previous content. AI can better mimic a consistent style when it has existing material as a guide.
3. **Adjust Tone in Prompts:** If AI content needs more personality, add tone-specific prompts like "Use a friendly and inviting tone" or "Make the content sound professional and confident."
4. **Regularly Update AI Content Examples:** Update the AI with your latest brand-representative content every few months to align with any shifts in tone or new content formats.

Example of Brand Voice Adjustment:

- **Original AI Draft:** "Our new eco-friendly water bottles are a must-have! They're designed with your health and the environment in mind."
- **Edited for Tone Consistency:** "Our eco-friendly water bottles aren't just a purchase—they're a commitment to your health and our planet. Choose sustainability every sip of the way."

5.3 Refining AI Outputs to Match Your Brand's Tone

Fine-tuning tone is essential to ensure AI-generated content resonates with your audience. Here's how to adjust the tone for three common brand types:

- **Professional and Authoritative:** Edit language to be precise, direct, and fact-based. Avoid overly casual language.

- **Example:** Replace "great choice for anyone" with "an ideal solution for professionals."
- **Conversational and Friendly:** Use a more relaxed tone, contractions, and inclusive language.
- **Example:** Replace "This product is beneficial" with "You'll love how easy this product makes your life."
- **Inspirational and Supportive:** Add motivational language and empathy to connect emotionally.
- **Example:** Replace "Our program provides solutions" with "We're here to support you every step of the way."

Exercise: Tone Adjustment Practice

Take a paragraph of AI-generated content and edit it to match your brand's tone. Experiment with different word choices and sentence structures until it aligns with your voice.

5.4 Cross-Checking Facts and Figures

While AI can generate content quickly, it can sometimes include inaccurate information. Always fact-check data, statistics, and any industry-specific information.

Tips for Verifying Accuracy:

1. **Use Trusted Sources:** Confirm details using reliable industry sources, like government reports, academic studies, or reputable news sites.
2. **Check Product and Service Details:** Ensure product descriptions or service information are up-to-date and accurate.

CHAPTER 5: REVIEWING AND EDITING AI CONTENT

3. **Adjust Prompt Instructions if Needed:** If accuracy is a recurring issue, add prompts like "Use only verifiable facts" or "Include up-to-date statistics."

Example of Fact-Checking AI Content:

- **AI Output:** "Our product has been clinically tested in over 50 studies."
- **Edited for Accuracy:** Verify the claim with your product team, and adjust if needed: "Our product has been rigorously tested to ensure top quality and reliability."

5.5 Adding Personal Touches to AI-Generated Content

AI drafts can often lack personal anecdotes or specific brand insights. Adding these human elements makes content feel more authentic and relatable.

Ways to Add Personalization:

1. **Share Brand Stories or Experiences:** Integrate your brand's journey or unique experiences related to the content.
2. **Include Customer Testimonials or Case Studies:** Real-life examples add credibility and help connect with your audience.
3. **Add Unique Insights:** If you have an expert opinion or insider knowledge, include it to make the content more valuable.

Example of Adding a Personal Touch:

- **AI Output:** "Exercise is a great way to stay healthy."
- **Edited for Personalization:** "At our studio, we believe exercise should be enjoyable. Our members often say our classes are the highlight of their week, helping them feel energized and strong."

5.6 Proofreading and Finalizing Content for Publication

The final stage of editing is proofreading, ensuring that content is free of errors and formatted for easy readability. AI tools like Grammarly or Hemingway Editor can assist with grammar and clarity, but a manual review is essential for the best results.

Proofreading Checklist:

- **Grammar and Spelling:** Correct any grammar, spelling, and punctuation errors.
- **Readability:** Ensure sentences are concise and content is easy to understand.
- **Formatting:** Add subheadings, bullet points, or short paragraphs for readability, especially in blog posts and emails.
- **Consistency:** Confirm consistency in terminology, formatting, and style.
- **Platform-Specific Edits:** Adjust for platform specifications (e.g., Instagram caption length, email preview text).

5.7 Practical Exercises for Editing Skills

Exercise 1: Tone Adjustment Practice

- Take a short AI-generated piece of content, such as a

product description, and edit it for different tones (e.g., professional, conversational, inspirational).
- Compare the edits to see which tone aligns best with your brand.

Exercise 2: Fact-Checking Practice

- Choose a paragraph with statistics or product claims from AI content. Research each fact to confirm its accuracy, adjusting the content where needed.

Exercise 3: Personalization Practice

- Select an AI draft (like an email or social media post) and add a brand-specific story or customer testimonial to make it feel more personalized and engaging.

Chapter Summary: Key Takeaways and Exercises

Key Takeaways:

- Establish a clear editing process to ensure AI content is high quality and aligned with brand standards.
- Maintain consistency in tone and style by refining AI prompts and adjusting outputs.
- Cross-check all facts and data to ensure accuracy, and add personal touches for a relatable, humanized feel.
- Proofread carefully to polish AI content for publication, ensuring readability and error-free language.

Exercises:

1. **Editing Process Practice:** Choose an AI draft and apply the editing process outlined in this chapter, from initial review to final proofreading.
2. **Tone and Voice Refinement:** Experiment with editing the tone of an AI-generated piece. Create three different versions: one professional, one conversational, and one inspirational.
3. **Content Personalization:** Take a generic piece of AI content and add your brand's unique perspective, stories, or testimonials to make it distinctive and authentic.

6

Chapter 6: Advanced AI Techniques

With a foundation in content creation and editing, it's time to explore the advanced capabilities of AI for marketing. Beyond generating content, AI can help analyse customer behavior, personalize interactions, segment audiences, and optimize content for better engagement. This chapter dives into these advanced applications, showing how to use AI to make marketing decisions driven by data and tailored to your audience's needs.

6.1 Leveraging AI Analytics for Content Optimization

AI analytics provide insights into how your content performs, helping you understand what resonates with your audience and where to improve. By analysing engagement metrics, AI can identify patterns in customer behavior and highlight content that drives the most value.

Steps for Using AI Analytics:

1. **Track Key Performance Indicators (KPIs):** Identify the

KPIs relevant to your marketing goals, such as click-through rates (CTR), time on page, and conversion rates.
2. **Analyse Audience Engagement:** Use AI tools to analyse how your audience interacts with different types of content, including blog posts, social media, and email.
3. **Content Testing and Feedback:** Test various content styles, formats, and topics, and analyse results to refine future content creation.

Example: Optimizing Blog Content

- **AI Insight:** AI analytics reveal that list-style blog posts with a conversational tone perform best.
- **Action:** Create more list-based posts and experiment with different tones to align with audience preferences.

AI Tools for Analytics: Google Analytics, HubSpot, and social media insights (e.g., Facebook and Instagram Analytics) are powerful tools for tracking engagement and AI-powered suggestions for optimizing content.

6.2 Using AI for Audience Insights and Personalization

Personalized marketing increases engagement by making content more relevant to individual customers. AI can analyse customer data to provide insights into customer preferences, allowing you to personalize your messaging.

Techniques for AI-Driven Personalization:

1. **Audience Segmentation:** Use AI to group customers based

on behaviour's, interests, or demographics, making it easier to create tailored messages for each segment.
2. **Behavioural Targeting:** Target content based on customers' past interactions, like browsing history, purchase behaviour, and email engagement.
3. **Predictive Analytics:** AI can forecast customer behaviour, such as the likelihood of making a purchase or churning, enabling proactive marketing strategies.

Example: Personalized Email Campaigns

- **Scenario:** A fitness brand segments customers into "beginners" and "advanced users."
- **Action:** AI generates tailored emails with beginner-friendly workout tips for new users and advanced training guides for experienced customers, boosting engagement by catering to their needs.

6.3 Automating Customer Segmentation and Targeted Messaging

Customer segmentation allows you to deliver more relevant content by categorizing your audience into specific groups. With AI, this process can be automated, saving time and increasing accuracy.

Steps for Automating Customer Segmentation:

1. **Define Segmentation Criteria:** Decide how you want to group customers—by demographics, past purchases, behavior, or engagement level.

2. **Set Up AI-Driven Segmentation Tools:** AI tools like CRM platforms can automate the segmentation process, ensuring customers are sorted in real-time based on evolving data.
3. **Implement Targeted Campaigns:** Use segmented data to send personalized emails, social media ads, or website content tailored to each group's interests.

Example: Targeted Social Media Ads

- **Scenario:** A skincare brand segments users by skin type.
- **Action:** AI creates targeted social media ads for each segment, such as products for sensitive skin or acne-prone skin, resulting in higher ad relevance and improved click-through rates.

AI Tools for Segmentation and Targeted Messaging: Tools like Salesforce, HubSpot, and Mailchimp provide AI-powered segmentation capabilities that enable personalized marketing at scale.

6.4 Automating Content Distribution Across Channels

AI can automate content distribution, allowing you to reach your audience consistently across multiple platforms without manual posting. By scheduling and adjusting content to optimize timing, AI streamlines multi-channel marketing.

Best Practices for AI-Driven Content Distribution:

1. **Choose Key Channels:** Identify the platforms where your

CHAPTER 6: ADVANCED AI TECHNIQUES

audience is most active, such as social media, email, or your website.
2. **Automate Scheduling:** Use AI tools to schedule content distribution based on peak engagement times. Tools like Buffer and Hootsuite offer insights on optimal posting schedules.
3. **Monitor and Adjust:** AI can track the performance of distributed content and suggest adjustments in timing or messaging for better results.

Example: Multi-Channel Campaign for Product Launch

- **Scenario:** A fashion brand launches a new collection.
- **Action:** AI schedules posts across Instagram, Facebook, and email, with each platform receiving tailored messaging. The system tracks engagement and optimizes timing for future posts.

6.5 Using AI for A/B Testing and Content Experimentation

A/B testing allows you to experiment with different content variations to see what resonates best with your audience. AI can streamline this process by creating multiple content versions and tracking their performance.

Steps for AI-Powered A/B Testing:

1. **Define Variables to Test:** Choose elements like headline, CTA, tone, or content format.
2. **Generate Variants:** AI can generate several content versions based on your parameters, such as different headline

styles or email subject lines.
3. **Analyse Results:** Use AI to track the performance of each variant, helping you make data-driven decisions on what content works best.

Example: Testing Email Subject Lines

- **Scenario:** A travel agency wants to increase email open rates.
- **Action:** AI generates two subject lines, one emphasizing discounts and another focusing on travel experiences. After testing, AI determines the more engaging approach, helping the agency optimize future campaigns.

AI Tools for A/B Testing: Tools like Google Optimize and Optimizely offer AI-driven A/B testing and performance insights.

6.6 Advanced Audience Targeting with AI Predictive Analytics

Predictive analytics enables you to anticipate customer behaviour's, such as the likelihood of purchase or attrition, by analysing past actions. By integrating predictive insights, you can proactively address customer needs and improve retention.

Techniques for Predictive Audience Targeting:

1. **Analyse Purchase Likelihood:** AI identifies which customers are likely to buy, allowing you to target them with specific offers.
2. **Identify At-Risk Customers:** Predictive analytics can flag customers who might churn, enabling you to send re-engagement messages.

3. **Personalize Recommendations:** Use past behaviour to provide product or content recommendations that align with customer interests.

Example: Retention Campaign for At-Risk Customers

- **Scenario:** An online subscription service identifies users with declining engagement.
- **Action:** AI sends these users a personalized email with a discount offer to encourage renewal, helping reduce churn and increase retention.

AI Tools for Predictive Analytics: Predictive analytics platforms like IBM Watson and Google Cloud AI offer powerful solutions for analysing customer behaviour's and targeting effectively.

6.7 Integrating AI with CRM Systems for Enhanced Customer Interactions

Customer Relationship Management (CRM) platforms can integrate with AI to enhance customer interactions, manage data, and improve response times.

Steps for Integrating AI with CRM:

1. **Centralize Customer Data:** Use a CRM platform to gather customer data in one place, from purchase history to social interactions.
2. **Automate Customer Communication:** AI-driven CRM can automate responses to inquiries, schedule follow-ups, and recommend products.

3. **Track Customer Satisfaction:** CRM data integrated with AI can analyse feedback trends, helping you adjust your strategy based on customer sentiment.

Example: AI-Powered Customer Support

- **Scenario:** An e-commerce brand uses AI-powered chatbots integrated with their CRM.
- **Action:** Chatbots handle routine questions, provide order updates, and suggest related products, resulting in faster support and improved customer satisfaction.

AI-Enhanced CRM Tools: Salesforce Einstein, Zoho CRM, and HubSpot's AI integrations offer CRM solutions that can elevate customer service and engagement with AI capabilities.

6.8 Automating Feedback Collection and Analysis with AI

Feedback is vital for improving products and services, and AI can automate its collection and analysis, revealing valuable insights into customer preferences.

Steps for Using AI to Analyse Customer Feedback:

1. **Collect Feedback Across Channels:** Use surveys, email responses, and social media comments to gather customer input.
2. **Analyse Sentiment:** AI tools can detect positive, negative, or neutral sentiments in feedback, providing insights into customer satisfaction.
3. **Identify Common Themes:** AI can categorize feedback by

theme, such as "product quality" or "customer service," helping you address specific areas.

Example: Product Improvement Based on Feedback

- **Scenario:** A food delivery service uses AI to analyse customer feedback, identifying frequent complaints about delivery times.
- **Action:** The company improves logistics based on these insights, leading to faster delivery and higher customer satisfaction.

Tools for Feedback Collection and Analysis: Tools like Qualtrics, MonkeyLearn, and IBM Watson Natural Language Understanding are equipped to automate feedback analysis and uncover actionable insights.

Chapter Summary: Key Takeaways and Exercises

Key Takeaways:

- AI analytics and predictive insights enable data-driven content optimization and personalized marketing.
- Automating segmentation, targeting, and A/B testing can save time and increase content relevance.
- Integrating AI with CRM systems enhances customer service and personalizes customer journeys.
- Feedback collection and sentiment analysis with AI provide insights for continuous improvement.

Exercises:

1. **Audience Segmentation Practice:** Use AI to segment your audience into at least three categories based on demographics or behaviour. Create personalized content for each segment.
2. **A/B Testing Experiment:** Set up an A/B test with AI-generated content, such as email subject lines or social media captions. Review the performance and adjust your strategy accordingly.
3. **Predictive Analytics Practice:** Identify a specific customer behaviour (e.g., likelihood of purchase) and create a strategy using AI to target these customers with relevant content.

7

Chapter 7: Real-Life Case Studies and Exercises

Real-life case studies illustrate the transformative potential of AI in marketing, showcasing how businesses of various sizes and industries use AI to streamline operations, engage customers, and drive growth. In this chapter, we'll explore several case studies that highlight different AI applications, followed by hands-on exercises to reinforce your learning and help you apply AI techniques in practical scenarios.

7.1 Case Studies: How Businesses Use AI for Marketing Success

These case studies highlight different approaches businesses take to leverage AI, from personalized email marketing to automated customer support. Each case study provides insights into the specific AI tools, strategies, and results, demonstrating the versatility of AI in real-world marketing.

Here are some real-world examples of companies effectively leveraging AI in their marketing efforts, each illustrating

unique applications that align with different objectives:

1. Netflix – Personalized Recommendations

   - Industry: Entertainment
   - Application: Personalization through recommendation algorithms
   - Details: Netflix uses AI to analyse viewing patterns and user interactions to suggest personalized content. This recommendation engine, powered by machine learning, analyses vast amounts of user data to predict what users are most likely to watch, keeping them engaged on the platform.
   - Impact: Estimated to drive over $1 billion annually by enhancing user engagement and reducing churn – Source material from HubSpot Blog

2. Sephora – AI Chatbot for Personalized Customer Experience

   - Industry: Retail (Beauty)
   - Application: AI-powered virtual artist and chatbot for personalized shopping experiences
   - Details: Sephora's Virtual Artist uses facial recognition and machine learning to help customers try on makeup virtually. Additionally, a chatbot provides personalized product recommendations and answers customer queries, simulating the experience of an in-store beauty advisor.
   - Impact: Increased customer satisfaction and conversion rates, as users engaged with the Virtual Artist were more likely to make a purchase

CHAPTER 7: REAL-LIFE CASE STUDIES AND EXERCISES

Source material from - AI & Digital Marketing Blog

3. Coca-Cola – "Masterpiece" AI Campaign

- Industry: Beverages
- Application: Generative AI for creative advertising
- Details: Coca-Cola's "Masterpiece" campaign uses generative AI to animate famous works of art, blending live-action and AI-generated visuals. Partnering with OpenAI's DALL-E and ChatGPT, Coca-Cola created an engaging digital ad that showcased the brand's creativity.
- Impact: Boosted brand engagement and highlighted Coca-Cola's innovative brand identity, drawing attention across social media

Source material from - The Keen Folks

4. Starbucks – Deep Brew for Personalized Offers

- Industry: Food and Beverage
- Application: AI-driven loyalty program and personalized marketing
- Details: Starbucks utilizes its proprietary AI system, Deep Brew, to create personalized offers for customers. It analyses purchase behaviour and visit times to send customized deals, encouraging app users to join its rewards program and increasing loyalty.
- Impact: Attracted over 4 million new loyalty members, significantly enhancing customer engagement and revenue

Source material - LocaliQ

5. Nike – Virtual Match between Two Eras of Serena Williams

- Industry: Sportswear
- Application: AI for video content creation and digital engagement
- Details: Nike used AI to create a simulated tennis match between virtual versions of Serena Williams from different eras (1999 vs. 2017). This campaign celebrated Serena's career while showcasing Nike's commitment to innovative storytelling, using AI to analyse her playing style across decades.
- Impact: Generated extensive media buzz, with the video viewed by millions, reinforcing Nike's position as a leader in digital marketing creativity

Source material - The Keen Folks

6. Unilever – AI in Social Media Advertising

- Industry: Consumer Goods
- Application: AI-optimized social media advertising
- Details: Unilever collaborated with an AI partner to analyse data from social platforms and identify the most effective ad formats for different demographics. AI was also used to create a personalized shopping assistant, improving customer experience and targeted ad performance.
- Impact: Improved advertising engagement by up to 50%, with optimized campaigns leading to higher ROI

CHAPTER 7: REAL-LIFE CASE STUDIES AND EXERCISES

Source material - AI & Digital Marketing Blog

These examples demonstrate how diverse industries can effectively integrate AI to personalize customer interactions, streamline content creation, and enhance advertising strategies. Each case underscores AI's potential to drive customer engagement, improve operational efficiency, and yield measurable results across various marketing applications.

7.2 Hands-On Exercises for Applying AI in Marketing

These exercises will help reinforce the concepts and strategies from the case studies and previous chapters. Each exercise is designed to be actionable, allowing you to practice AI applications for content creation, audience segmentation, and customer engagement.

Exercise 1: Social Media Content Creation with AI

Objective: Practice using AI to generate social media content ideas and captions.

1. **Define Your Theme:** Choose a theme for the month (e.g., sustainability, customer stories, product tips).
2. **Prompt AI for Content Ideas:** Use prompts like "Create a week's worth of social media posts on [theme]" or "Write Instagram captions that promote our new eco-friendly products."
3. **Review and Edit:** Go through the AI-generated content and adjust tone, language, or details to align with your brand.

Outcome: Create a social media content plan for one week, including caption drafts and ideas for images or hashtags.

Exercise 2: Personalizing Email Content with AI

Objective: Generate segmented email content using AI.

1. **Segment Your Audience:** Divide your customers into at least two groups (e.g., new customers and returning customers).
2. **Create Targeted Prompts:** For each segment, create a prompt such as "Write a welcome email for new customers introducing our brand and offering a discount code" and "Draft an email for loyal customers, highlighting our new product line and thanking them for their continued support."
3. **Adjust Tone and Personalization:** Edit the emails for tone, add personalization, and ensure each email reflects the recipient's needs.

Outcome: Draft personalized emails for two different customer segments, enhancing relevance and engagement.

Exercise 3: Customer Support with AI Chatbots

Objective: Outline a set of responses for a basic AI chatbot to handle common customer inquiries.

1. **Identify Common Inquiries:** Make a list of the top five questions your customers frequently ask (e.g., "What is your return policy?" "How can I track my order?").

2. **Create Response Prompts:** Write prompts for each question like "Provide a response explaining our return policy" or "Give instructions on how to track an order."
3. **Test and Refine Responses:** Use AI to generate responses and edit them to ensure they are clear, accurate, and consistent with your brand's tone.

Outcome: A basic FAQ-style response library for a chatbot, reducing the workload for your customer support team.

Exercise 4: Creating Segmented Ad Copy

Objective: Practice generating ad copy tailored to different customer segments.

1. **Define Segments and Goals:** Choose two customer segments (e.g., "health-conscious parents" and "young professionals").
2. **Prompt AI for Ad Copy:** For each segment, create prompts like "Write a Facebook ad targeting health-conscious parents, promoting our organic snack packs for kids" and "Generate an Instagram ad for young professionals, highlighting our healthy ready-to-eat meal options."
3. **Edit and Test:** Review AI-generated ad copy, adjust for tone, and prepare it for testing on your chosen platform.

Outcome: Two sets of ad copy tailored to different segments, ready for A/B testing on social media.

Exercise 5: Analysing Customer Feedback with AI

Objective: Use AI to interpret customer feedback for actionable insights.

1. **Collect Feedback:** Gather a sample of customer reviews, survey responses, or social media comments.
2. **Prompt AI for Sentiment Analysis:** Use a prompt like "Analyse these customer reviews for common themes and sentiment."
3. **Identify Key Insights:** Summarize the main points, such as "positive feedback on product quality" or "requests for faster shipping," and identify areas for improvement.

Outcome: An analysis of customer feedback with actionable insights for product or service enhancements.

Chapter Summary: Key Takeaways and Exercises

Key Takeaways:

- Real-life case studies showcase the versatility of AI across various marketing functions, from content creation to customer support.
- AI-driven segmentation, personalized email marketing, and social media engagement can significantly improve customer experience and boost engagement.
- Hands-on exercises help reinforce skills, enabling you to apply AI techniques in practical business scenarios.

Exercises:

1. **Social Media Content Plan:** Use AI to create a week's worth of social media content focused on a specific theme.

2. **Segmented Email Creation:** Draft personalized emails for at least two audience segments using AI-generated prompts.
3. **Chatbot Response Library:** Develop a basic response set for an AI chatbot to handle FAQs.
4. **Targeted Ad Copy Practice:** Generate and refine ad copy for distinct customer segments using AI.
5. **Customer Feedback Analysis:** Use AI to analyse and extract insights from customer feedback, identifying trends and improvement areas.

8

Chapter 8: Ethical and Practical Considerations in AI Marketing

As AI becomes more integral to marketing, it's essential to consider ethical implications and practical guidelines to use these tools responsibly. Ethical AI marketing builds trust with customers, respects privacy, and ensures that automation complements rather than replaces human interaction. This chapter explores best practices for responsible AI use, strategies to maintain a personal touch, and practical steps to balance automation with authenticity.

8.1 The Importance of Ethical AI in Marketing

Ethical AI practices are vital for building and maintaining trust with your audience. Misuse of AI—whether through data privacy breaches, biased content generation, or impersonal automated interactions—can lead to customer mistrust and even legal challenges. Ethical AI in marketing includes using data responsibly, ensuring content transparency, and prioritizing fair and inclusive messaging.

Key Areas of Ethical Consideration:

- **Data Privacy and Consent:** Customers expect their personal data to be handled securely and with transparency. Comply with privacy regulations like GDPR and CCPA, and obtain explicit consent before collecting data.
- **Transparency and Honesty:** Make it clear when content is AI-generated, especially in areas like customer service chatbots or automated emails. Honesty about AI's role in your business helps build customer trust.
- **Avoiding Bias and Ensuring Inclusivity:** AI models may inadvertently produce biased outputs based on the data they are trained on. Regularly review AI-generated content for fairness and inclusivity to ensure it doesn't alienate or misrepresent any group.

8.2 Data Privacy and Compliance in AI Marketing

AI marketing relies heavily on customer data for insights and personalization, making data privacy a top priority. Ensuring compliance with data protection regulations like GDPR in the EU or CCPA in California helps protect customer information and demonstrates responsible data practices.

Best Practices for Data Privacy Compliance:

1. **Obtain Clear Consent:** Before collecting or using customer data, get explicit consent. Include clear options to opt-in or opt-out of data collection.
2. **Limit Data Collection:** Collect only the data you need for specific marketing purposes. Avoid gathering unnecessary

personal information.
3. **Use Data Anonymization:** When possible, anonymize data to prevent identifying individual customers, which reduces the risk in case of a data breach.
4. **Regularly Audit Data Security Measures:** Implement strong cybersecurity protocols to safeguard customer information, and conduct regular security audits to check for vulnerabilities.

Example: When using AI for personalized email campaigns, ensure customers have consented to receive marketing emails and have access to opt-out options in each communication.

8.3 Balancing Automation with a Human Touch

While AI can streamline many marketing tasks, maintaining a personal touch is crucial to prevent interactions from feeling robotic or impersonal. Customers value genuine, human-centered interactions, especially when dealing with customer service or complex inquiries.

Strategies to Balance AI with Human Interaction:

1. **Combine AI with Human Oversight:** Use AI to handle repetitive tasks, such as initial customer inquiries, and involve human agents for more complex issues. This balance ensures efficiency without sacrificing personalized support.
2. **Humanize Automated Content:** Make automated emails, social media posts, and chatbot responses feel more personable. Small adjustments, like friendly language or

personalization tokens (e.g., using the customer's name), can make a big difference.
3. **Allow Easy Access to Human Support:** In customer service scenarios, always offer an option to connect with a human agent if the customer prefers.

Example: A chatbot on an e-commerce site can handle FAQs, but it should also allow customers to speak with a human if the question goes beyond routine inquiries, creating a balanced and satisfying customer experience.

8.4 AI Transparency and Customer Trust

Transparency in how AI is used builds customer trust. Customers appreciate knowing when they are interacting with AI and why their data is being used. This clarity fosters transparency and ensures customers feel respected and informed.

Best Practices for AI Transparency:

1. **Label AI Interactions Clearly:** Let customers know when they are interacting with an AI, whether it's a chatbot, a recommendation engine, or an automated email.
2. **Explain Data Use Policies:** Clearly outline how customer data is used to improve AI-driven services, such as personalized recommendations. Make your privacy policies easily accessible.
3. **Acknowledge AI's Role in Content Creation:** If significant portions of content, such as product descriptions or blogs, are AI-generated, consider including a note stating the role of AI. This can help manage customer expectations.

Example: A customer support chatbot can include a line like, "I'm here to help answer your questions quickly. If you need a human touch, just let me know!"

8.5 Avoiding Bias in AI Content

AI tools are trained on large datasets, which can sometimes contain biases that lead to unintended messaging. By actively monitoring and refining AI outputs, businesses can create more fair, inclusive, and respectful content that reflects diverse perspectives.

Strategies for Identifying and Mitigating Bias:

1. **Regularly Review AI Content:** Periodically assess AI-generated content for potential bias, including language that may inadvertently exclude or misrepresent groups.
2. **Train AI on Diverse Data Sources:** Ensure AI models are trained on a wide range of data to reduce inherent biases.
3. **Invite Feedback from Diverse Perspectives:** Encourage team members from various backgrounds to review AI content, bringing different perspectives to identify and eliminate bias.

Example: If AI is used to write customer profiles or target specific audiences, regularly review outputs to ensure they are free of stereotypes or assumptions.

8.6 Ensuring Content Authenticity with AI

AI can automate content creation, but too much automation

risks diluting your brand's authenticity. Authenticity is key to customer loyalty, so it's essential to keep your brand's unique voice intact.

Techniques to Maintain Authenticity:

1. **Blend AI with Original Content:** Use AI for initial drafts, topic ideas, or content outlines, and add a human touch in the final edit to keep the content authentic.
2. **Incorporate Unique Brand Stories:** Sharing real stories, testimonials, or personal insights adds depth and authenticity, making content more relatable.
3. **Personalize Interactions Thoughtfully:** Avoid over-automation. Aim for genuine personalization by using customer names, preferences, or previous purchases where relevant.

Example: An AI-generated blog draft can be edited to include a personal anecdote or specific examples relevant to your brand's journey, maintaining a relatable and unique voice.

8.7 Monitoring and Auditing AI for Continuous Improvement

To ensure that AI tools remain effective and ethical, regular monitoring and auditing are essential. By evaluating AI performance and staying updated on new AI features and capabilities, you can adapt your strategy for the best results.

Steps for Monitoring and Auditing AI:

1. **Set Key Performance Indicators (KPIs):** Establish KPIs to

track the success of AI-driven initiatives, such as engagement rates, customer satisfaction, or response times.
2. **Conduct Regular Audits:** Periodically review AI content, accuracy, and customer interactions to ensure they meet your standards and are free of bias.
3. **Update AI with Fresh Data:** Continuously provide new data to AI models to help them stay current with your audience's evolving preferences and interests.
4. **Stay Updated on AI Best Practices:** Keep abreast of ethical AI guidelines, regulatory updates, and emerging technologies to maintain compliance and enhance performance.

Example: If an AI tool is used for email segmentation, regularly audit the segmentation accuracy and customer response metrics to ensure the AI remains effective and aligned with audience needs.

8.8 Future-Proofing Your AI Strategy

AI technology evolves rapidly, so it's essential to stay adaptable. Future-proofing your AI strategy ensures you can integrate new advancements, adapt to regulatory changes, and continue to meet customer expectations.

Tips for Future-Proofing AI Strategy:

1. **Invest in Scalable AI Tools:** Choose AI tools and platforms that can scale with your business and integrate new features as they are released.
2. **Commit to Continuous Learning:** Stay informed about AI advancements and training opportunities to keep your

team updated on best practices.
3. **Engage in Responsible AI Communities:** Many organizations and industry groups provide resources on ethical AI usage. Participating in these communities can offer insights and keep your AI strategy compliant and forward-thinking.

Example: As more platforms incorporate AI for personalized customer journeys, consider implementing tools that allow flexibility to adapt to new customer expectations and industry trends.

Chapter Summary: Key Takeaways and Exercises

Key Takeaways:

- Ethical AI practices, including data privacy, transparency, and inclusivity, build customer trust and ensure responsible AI use.
- Balancing automation with human interaction maintains a personal touch, essential for customer loyalty.
- Regular monitoring and auditing of AI tools can prevent bias, improve accuracy, and keep content relevant.
- Future-proofing your AI strategy by investing in scalable tools and staying updated on best practices prepares you for continued AI success.

Exercises:

1. **Data Privacy Audit:** Review your data privacy policies and ensure they comply with relevant regulations (e.g., GDPR,

CCPA). Check that customers have clear consent options for data collection.

2. **Bias Check Exercise:** Choose a sample of AI-generated content and review it for potential biases. Edit any language or concepts that might unintentionally exclude or misrepresent groups.

3. **Transparency Exercise:** Add a line of transparency in one AI interaction (e.g., a chatbot message) explaining its AI nature. Review customer reactions to gauge the impact on trust.

4. **Authenticity Check:** Take a piece of AI-generated content, such as a blog post, and add brand-specific anecdotes or insights to make it more authentic and aligned with your brand voice.

5. **AI Performance Audit:** Select a specific AI function, such as email segmentation or chatbot responses, and review its performance metrics. Identify areas for improvement based on customer feedback or engagement data.

9

Conclusion: Embracing AI Responsibly for Marketing Success

This instructional guide equips readers with the knowledge to integrate AI tools thoughtfully and effectively into their marketing strategy. By following these best practices, business owners can harness AI's potential to create meaningful customer experiences, streamline operations, and drive business growth.

If you need help with AI or software development please contact www.digitalsolutions.help

About the Author

Master AI Marketing

At Digital Solutions, our journey as software and mobile app developers has shown us the growing demand for AI integration in businesses. Recognizing this, we developed this book as a guide to help our clients once their software and apps are in place and any company understand how to leverage AI for effective marketing strategies. This resource provides actionable insights tailored for businesses ready to adopt AI-driven marketing solutions for growth and customer engagement. If you need more information on AI, software and mobile app development, scan the QR code or visit www.digitalsolutions.help.

You can connect with me on:
🌐 https://www.digitalsolutions.help

Also by Evanthia & Rob Steadman

The Unbelieving Heroes
Ethan has always been the level-headed, sensible type, but his reality starts unravelling when strange, unexplainable events begin happening around him. Buildings change colours, people act oddly, and he starts seeing bizarre, god-like figures who seem to treat Earth as a playground. When he tries to share his concerns, his best friend Max—a charismatic ladies' man with little patience for supernatural theories—brushes it off, convinced it's all in Ethan's head.

However, the duo eventually comes face-to-face with the powerful aliens, who mock humanity and appear to warp reality purely for their amusement. Frustrated but determined, Ethan and Max dig deeper and accidentally stumble upon the aliens' unlikely weakness.

www.ingramcontent.com/pod-product-compliance
Lightning Source LLC
Chambersburg PA
CBHW070121230526
45472CB00004B/1365